WILLIAMS-SONOMA

Sweet Treats

recipes
carolyn beth weil

general editor
chuck williams

photography
jason lowe

fP
FREE PRESS

NEW YORK · LONDON · TORONTO · SYDNEY

contents

* For a complete list of recipes, turn to page 128.

15

kid classics

33

baked
delights

87

frozen
wonders

105

favorite
beverages

hey kids!

This book shows you how fun and easy baking can be! There are times when you need to pay attention, like when you are using knives, cooking on the stove top, and baking in the oven. But don't worry, all you need to remember are two key words: sharp and hot. Whenever those words come to mind, ask an adult to stand by. They can be really helpful (and may even wash the dishes!).

Here are some secrets to cooking success:

* Read the Basics section first.

* Before you begin any recipe, read it from start to finish.

* Look for the splats over the numbers in the recipe steps. These will tell you which picture goes with each step.

Beyond that, all that's left to do is to start cooking and have some fun!

hey parents!

The recipes in this cookbook are intended for kids age 8 and up, to use with as much independence as seems right for their age and skill level. Only you can gauge how much support you will need to give to your children as they cook. Help your children by reviewing the recipe with them before they begin and identifying any steps that may require adult supervision.

getting started

Before you begin to bake, make sure an adult is around to help out. If you have long hair, tie it back. Take off any dangling things like scarves, hair ribbons, or jewelry that could catch on fire, fall into a pan, or get tangled. Roll up long sleeves and put on an apron.

clear your work surface

The next thing you need is a clean work surface. Before the fun begins, clear off a big, flat area, such as a kitchen counter or table, to work on. Wipe down the surface to make sure it's clean. Then, wash and dry your hands thoroughly.

assemble your supplies

Restaurant pastry chefs are well organized and always gather their equipment and prepare their ingredients ahead of time, a system called *mise en place* (pronounced MEEZ ahn plahse), meaning "everything in its place."

Take a look at the list of equipment and ingredients for the recipe you are making. Get out your tools first. Then, get out all the ingredients you're going to need. Ingredients combine better at room temperature, so let cold items from the refrigerator warm up for no longer than 1 hour before using them, unless the recipe says otherwise.

Next, peel and chop your fruits, nuts, or chocolate, and measure out all the ingredients. If the recipe calls for using the oven, turn it on to the correct temperature before you start. To be sure your oven is at the right temperature, always "preheat" it for 10–15 minutes before you use it.

Many of the recipes in this book call for greasing a pan or dish before you fill it. This helps keep the food from sticking and makes cleanup easier. To do this, use a piece of paper towel to swab a small amount of softened butter, then rub it all over on the bottom of the pan and up the sides, if present.

preparing ingredients

washing fruit

Wash large fruit under slightly warm running water, gently rubbing the fruit all over. Put berries in a colander, gently rinse with cool water, then turn them out onto paper towels and let them air-dry.

zesting & juicing citrus

To remove the zest (the colored part) of a citrus fruit, grasp the citrus firmly and rub it over the grating teeth of a box grater-shredder using short strokes. Rub each surface only once and don't use too much pressure, or you'll dig into the bitter white pith underneath. Remember to wipe the zest from the back side of the grater.

To juice a citrus fruit, roll it under your palm a few times, then cut the fruit in half crosswise. Press the cut side of the fruit onto the pointy top of a citrus juicer. Turn the fruit half back and forth, giving it a good squeeze as you turn, to extract the juice.

chopping chocolate

On a clean, dry cutting board, place the chocolate piece flat. Holding the handle of a serrated knife in one hand, and pressing on top of the knife with your other hand, cut small chunks off the edge of the chocolate (this may require adult help). Chop the chunks into pieces no larger than peas.

cracking eggs

Tap an egg firmly on a flat surface until the shell cracks. Holding one end of the egg in each hand, pull the shell halves apart over a small bowl until the egg drops out into the bowl. Throw away the shell. Next, check for shell fragments: If a piece of shell drops into the bowl, chase it to the side of the bowl with a spoon, and then lift it out. Then, pour the egg into the mixing bowl.

Measuring spoons come in sets of ¼ teaspoon, ½ teaspoon, 1 teaspoon, and 1 tablespoon. The same spoons are used for dry and liquid ingredients.

how to measure dry ingredients

To measure dry ingredients such as flour or sugar, spoon the ingredient into the correct-sized dry measuring cup. Do not pack down the ingredient (unless it's brown sugar, which is measured firmly packed). Using the flat side of a table knife, sweep off the excess even with the rim. Gently scoop loose dry ingredients, such as raisins, into dry measuring cups just until the cup is full. To measure small amounts of dry ingredients, dip the correct-sized measuring spoon into the ingredient, then use the back of a table knife to sweep off the excess.

how to measure liquids

To measure liquid ingredients such as milk or lemon juice, set a clear liquid measuring cup on a flat surface, like a countertop. Pour the liquid into the cup. Now, scoot down so that your face is level with the cup and look at the measuring line for the amount you need. Does the level of the liquid match the correct line? If not, add more liquid (or pour some out) until the two lines are even. To measure a small amount of liquid, carefully pour the ingredient into a measuring spoon until it reaches the rim.

measuring

The recipes in this book will tell you how much of an ingredient you will need, then tell you whether you need to peel, chop, or grate it. Always use standard measuring cups and spoons for measuring. If an ingredient, such as sugar, comes in a range of measurements, it means you should taste and decide for yourself how much of the ingredient is needed.

types of measuring tools

It is especially important when baking to know the difference between dry and liquid measuring cups. Using the wrong type of cup could affect your recipe. Measuring cups for dry ingredients come in plastic or metal and in sets of ¼, ⅓, ½, and 1 cup. A liquid measuring cup is clear glass or plastic and has lines indicating amounts on the side.

knife skills

Whenever you're going to use a knife, ask an adult to help you. Always make sure your knife is sharp. Sharp knives are safer than dull knives because they cut cleanly and easily. You need to use a lot of pressure to cut with a dull knife, and it's more likely to slip or get stuck in what you're cutting. (You can hurt yourself with sharp knives too, of course, so use them with care.)

about cutting boards

Use a cutting board, made from wood or plastic, every time you cut. Other surfaces may be slippery, or they may dull your knife. It's best to keep separate cutting boards for fruits and vegetables and for raw meat, poultry, and fish to avoid spreading germs.

It may seem strange, but it's a good idea to smell your cutting board and check for strong odors before using it to chop fruit, chocolate, or other sweet items.

how to use a knife

✳ Pick a knife that fits comfortably in your hand and doesn't feel too big. Your hands are much smaller than an adult's. You can do the same job with a smaller tool.

✳ Hold the knife firmly by the handle. You can extend your index finger along the top or side of the blade to help guide the knife.

✳ Hold down the item you are cutting with your other hand, placing the food on a flat side whenever you can. (You can even cut a little slice off of a round thing to give it a stable flat side to sit on.)

✳ Curl under the fingers of the hand that's holding the food to keep them out of harm's way. You can use your knuckles as a shield to keep the blade from coming too close to your fingertips.

✳ Start to cut, always moving the knife away from your body as you do. The recipe will tell you whether to cut crosswise (across) or lengthwise (along the length).

food safety

Keeping the food you cook safe and healthful is mostly a matter of common sense. As your parents tell you: always wash your hands with hot water and soap before you start baking, after you finish, and frequently in the middle. Also, don't forget to wash before you sit down to eat.

keeping things clean & safe

Dairy products like milk, butter, and eggs can easily collect bacteria and spoil if left out of the refrigerator for too long. Some recipes specify that ingredients should be at room temperature before using. In this case, measure the amount of the ingredient called for, then leave just that amount out on the counter for no longer than 1 hour. Reduce the standing time in hot weather.

Remember to promptly wash any bowls, cutting boards, knives, and other utensils you used with hot, soapy water as soon as you are done with them.

Here are some more helpful hints for keeping your treats fresh and delicious:

✳ Never taste raw eggs, as they can sometimes contain bacteria that will make you sick. It's a good idea to wash your hands again each time you touch raw eggs.

✳ Germs, better known as bacteria, grow best in warm temperatures, so always keep hot foods hot and cold foods cold.

✳ Put things away as you go. Don't leave ingredients that should be refrigerated sitting out on the counter for more than 1 hour (less in hot weather).

✳ Don't put hot food straight into the refrigerator. This will raise the temperature in the refrigerator and may cause other foods stored there to spoil. Instead, let the hot food cool to room temperature before putting it into the fridge.

clean up as you bake

Good bakers know it's important to clean up as you go along. Don't save it all until the end. Put a dirty spoon in the sink or dishwasher instead of leaving it on the countertop. After you measure out an ingredient, put it away. Keep a clean dish towel or sponge handy for spills. Wipe down your work surface or cutting board often, and wash your hands whenever they get sticky.

start baking!

Before you turn on the oven or the stove, double-check to make sure an adult is nearby. Ask them to find you a sturdy chair or stool that you can safely stand on, so that you can see what's going on.

Baking in the oven or cooking on the stove top can sometimes seem scary, but don't let that stop you! Keep these final tips in mind, and you'll be well on your way to baking with confidence.

tips for working with hot things

✳ Always angle pot handles toward the back of the stove so you won't knock a pot off the stove by mistake. Never reach over an open flame.

✳ Never leave something cooking on the stove top unattended. If you need to leave the kitchen, be sure to turn off the burner and remove the pan from the heat.

✳ If you need to leave the kitchen while the oven is still on, be sure to let an adult know your plans.

✳ To protect your hands when working with hot items, always use clean, dry pot holders or oven mitts (oven mitts are nice because they act like gloves). Wet oven mitts will not protect you.

✳ Ask an adult to help you remove pans or dishes from the oven. Ask them to help you take large, hot pots off the stove, too.

✳ Tilt the lid away from you as you lift it off a hot pan. Steam is hotter than boiling water, which means it can burn you.

✳ Burners, especially electric ones, stay hot after you've turned them off. Never put anything that might get burnt onto a burner, including paper towels, cookbooks, oven mitts, or, of course, your hands.

✳ The inside of the oven door and the oven racks are very hot, so be careful not to touch them when checking on or removing your finished food.

✳ Remember to set a timer when baking. It's easy to get distracted by other things while your cookies are in the oven, so don't rely on your memory to remind you when the food will be ready.

✳ Have a cooling rack, heatproof trivet, or tile ready on a flat surface before you take a hot pan out of the oven or off the stove. Let hot pots and pans cool before putting them in the sink or cleaning them up.

✳ Remember to turn off the oven or burner after you are finished using it.

✳ Finally, remember to work slowly so you will avoid making mistakes.

You are now ready to choose a recipe and begin to bake. One last thing before you start: Above all, remember to have fun!

kid classics

lemon bars

ingredients

CRUST
all-purpose flour 1 cup
granulated sugar ¼ cup
salt ½ teaspoon
cold unsalted butter ½ cup (1 stick)

FILLING
lemon 1, scrubbed
large eggs 2, at room temperature
granulated sugar 1 cup
all-purpose flour 2 tablespoons
baking powder ½ teaspoon

powdered sugar for decoration

tools

measuring cups & spoons

8-inch square baking pan

parchment paper

small, medium & large bowls

whisk

cutting board & sharp knife

pastry blender

box grater-shredder

citrus juicer

electric mixer

oven mitts & cooling rack

rubber spatula

fine-mesh sieve

1 before you start

✳ Be sure an adult is nearby to help.

✳ Position an oven rack in the center of the oven. Preheat the oven to 350°F.

✳ Swab a small amount of butter onto a paper towel and rub it evenly over the bottom and sides of the baking pan.

✳ Line the baking pan with parchment, letting the paper hang over 2 sides of the pan.

2 mix the dry things

✳ In the medium bowl, use the whisk to stir together the flour, sugar, and salt until evenly blended.

3 cut in the butter

✳ Put the butter on the cutting board. Using the sharp knife, cut it into small cubes. Add the cubes to the bowl with the flour mixture.

✳ Using the pastry blender, make quick, firm chopping motions to cut the butter into the flour mixture until it looks like coarse crumbs, with some chunks the size of peas. This could take a while, so be patient.

4 form the crust

✳ Gather the butter-flour mixture together and pat it into the prepared baking pan, making an even layer. This will be the crust.

✳ Put the pan in the oven and bake until the crust is lightly golden, 15–20 minutes.

✳ While you are waiting for the crust to bake, go ahead and do steps 5 & 6.

5 prepare the lemon

✳ Holding the lemon over the cutting board, rub it over the small grating holes of the box grater-shredder. Use short strokes and turn the lemon as you work to rub off only the colored part of the peel (the zest). Measure out 1 teaspoon lemon zest and add it to the large bowl.

✳ Cut the lemons in half. Twist the lemon halves over the cone of the juicer to extract the juice. Pick out and throw away any seeds. Measure out 2 tablespoons juice and add it to the bowl with the zest.

6 make the filling

✻ Add the eggs and granulated sugar to the bowl with the lemon mixture. Using the electric mixer on low speed, beat the ingredients until well mixed. Increase the speed to high and beat until the mixture is pale and foamy, 1–2 minutes.

✻ Whisk together the flour and baking powder in the small bowl. Whisk the flour mixture into the lemon mixture.

7 bake the filling

✻ Ask an adult to help you remove the crust from the oven and place it on a heatproof surface.

✻ Carefully pour the lemon filling mixture over the hot crust, using the rubber spatula to scrape the bowl clean.

✻ Wearing oven mitts, return the pan to the oven and bake until the filling is set and lightly golden on top, 25–30 minutes.

8 cool & decorate

✻ Ask an adult to help you remove the pan from the oven and place it on the cooling rack. Let cool completely.

✻ Wipe the cutting board. Using both hands, lift the parchment to remove the cooled "cookie" from the pan and place it on the cutting board. Using the knife, cut the cookie into 16 square-shaped bars.

✻ Put the powdered sugar in the sieve, hold it over the bars, and tap the side to release the sugar in a thin layer over the lemon bars.

double-chocolate brownies

16 bars

ingredients

unsweetened chocolate 4 ounces

unsalted butter 1 cup (2 sticks)

sugar 2 cups

vanilla extract 2 teaspoons

large eggs 3, at room temperature

all-purpose flour 1 cup

salt ¼ teaspoon

chopped walnuts ½ cup

ICING

unsalted butter 6 tablespoons

semisweet chocolate chips 1 cup

tools

measuring cups & spoons

9-inch square baking pan

parchment paper

cutting board, serrated knife
& sharp knife

medium saucepan

heatproof rubber spatula

medium & small bowls

wooden spoon

thin bamboo skewer

oven mitts & cooling rack

offset icing spatula

1 before you start

✴ Be sure an adult is nearby to help.

✴ Position an oven rack in the center
of the oven. Preheat the oven to 350°F.

✴ Swab a small amount of butter on
a paper towel and rub it evenly over the
bottom and sides of the baking pan.

✴ Line the bottom of the baking pan
with parchment paper, letting the paper
hang over 2 sides of the pan.

2 melt the chocolate

✴ Put the chocolate and butter on the
cutting board. Use the serrated knife to chop
the chocolate into small bits. Next, cut the
butter into chunks.

✴ In the saucepan, combine the chocolate
and butter and place over medium-low
heat. Stir with the rubber spatula until the
chocolate and butter are melted and the
mixture is smooth. Chocolate burns easily,
so it is important to watch it closely.
Remove the pan from the heat.

kid classics **21**

problem?

✱ If your eggs are cold, or you beat them in all at once, your batter might separate and look curdled.

✱ Instead, make sure your eggs are at room temperature and beat them into the batter one at a time.

avoided!

3 make the batter

✱ Pour the chocolate mixture into the medium bowl, scraping out every last bit with the rubber spatula. Add the sugar and vanilla to the chocolate mixture and stir well with the wooden spoon.

✱ One at a time, crack the eggs into the small bowl and check for shells. Add the eggs to the batter, one at a time, beating well after adding each one.

✱ Add the flour and salt and stir until all the flour is mixed in. Then stir in the walnuts just until mixed.

4 bake the batter

✱ Using the rubber spatula, scrape the batter into the prepared baking pan. Spread it evenly in the pan and smooth the top. Put the pan in the oven.

✱ Bake the brownie for 40–45 minutes.

✱ To test if the brownie is done, ask an adult to help you pull out the oven rack and insert the skewer into the center of the brownie. It should come out clean. If the skewer is not clean, bake for 5 minutes longer and test again.

5 make the icing

✳ Ask an adult to help you remove the baking pan from the oven and place it on the cooling rack. Let it cool for 30 minutes.

✳ While the brownie cools, wash the bowl, saucepan, and rubber spatula.

✳ Put the butter on the cutting board and cut it into $1/2$-inch pieces with the sharp knife. Put the butter in the saucepan with the chocolate chips and melt them over medium-low heat the same way you did before. Stir with the rubber spatula until the mixture is smooth. This will be the icing.

6 ice the brownies

✳ Pour the icing over the top of the cooled brownie and use the offset icing spatula to help spread the icing evenly to the edges.

✳ Let the brownie stand for 30 minutes to set the icing. Chill until serving time.

7 cut & serve

✳ Wipe the cutting board. Carefully run the sharp knife along the edges of the pan that are not covered by the parchment. Use 2 hands to lift the parchment from the pan and place the brownie on the cutting board.

✳ Ask an adult to help you cut the brownie into 16 pieces. To do this, use the knife to cut it in half, then cut each half in half again, in the same direction; turn the brownie and repeat.

strawberry shortcakes

ingredients

all-purpose flour 2 cups

granulated sugar ¼ cup plus
1–2 tablespoons

baking powder 2 teaspoons

salt ¼ teaspoon

cold unsalted butter 6 tablespoons

heavy cream ¾ cup

strawberries 1 basket (2 cups)

WHIPPED CREAM
cold heavy cream 1 cup

granulated sugar 1 tablespoon

vanilla extract 1 teaspoon

powdered sugar for serving

tools

measuring cups & spoons

cookie sheet & parchment paper

small, medium & large bowls

whisk

sharp knife & cutting board

pastry blender

wooden spoon

rolling pin

3-inch biscuit cutter

oven mitts & cooling rack

electric mixer

small fine-mesh sieve

1 before you start

* Be sure an adult is nearby to help.

* Position an oven rack in the center of the oven. Preheat the oven to 375°F.

* Line the cookie sheet with a piece of parchment paper.

2 make the dough

* In the large bowl, use the whisk to stir together the flour, the ¼ cup sugar, the baking powder, and the salt until evenly blended. Cut the butter into small cubes and add them to the flour mixture.

* Using the pastry blender, make quick, firm chopping motions to cut the butter into the flour mixture until it looks like coarse crumbs, with some chunks the size of peas.

* Add the cream and stir with the wooden spoon until the dough starts to come together.

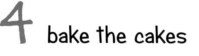

3 roll & cut the cakes

✳ Sprinkle a work surface with flour to keep the dough from sticking. Turn the dough out of the bowl and pat it into a disk. Roll it out with the rolling pin, giving the dough a quarter turn now and then, into a round slab that's 1 inch thick. Pat the sides to make them neat.

✳ Use the biscuit cutter to cut out 4 rounds. Gather the remaining dough together, roll it out again, just as you did before, and cut 2 more rounds.

4 bake the cakes

✳ Move the dough rounds to the cookie sheet. Put the cookie sheet in the oven and bake until the shortcakes are golden brown on top, 18–20 minutes.

✳ Ask an adult to help you remove the cookie sheet from the oven and put it on the cooling rack. Let the cakes cool for 10–15 minutes before assembling them.

5 prepare the berries

✳ While the shortcakes cool, put the strawberries on the cutting board. Pull or cut out the stem and white core from the center of each berry.

✳ Using the sharp knife, cut the strawberries into thin slices.

✳ Put the sliced berries in the medium bowl and sprinkle with the remaining 1–2 tablespoons sugar (the amount depends on how sweet the berries are— taste one!). Let the berries stand for 10 minutes.

problem?

✳ If you whip cream for too long, it will get very stiff and eventually turn into butter.

✳ Be sure to check the consistency of the cream often. Stop beating it while it still looks soft and pillowy and soft peaks form (see step 6).

avoided!

6 whip the cream

✳ Wash the large bowl. Put the cream, sugar, and vanilla extract in the bowl. Using the electric mixer, begin beating on low speed.

✳ When the cream begins to thicken and no longer splatters (this will take about 2 minutes), increase the mixer speed to medium-high.

✳ Continue to beat until the cream forms soft peaks that fall to one side when the beaters are lifted (turn off the mixer first!), which takes about 3 minutes.

7 build the shortcakes

✳ Ask an adult to help you split each cooled shortcake in half horizontally.

✳ Place the shortcake bottoms, cut side up, on serving plates and spoon the strawberries on top, dividing them equally. Add a big spoonful of whipped cream and top with the shortcake top.

✳ Put the powdered sugar in the sieve, hold it over the shortcakes, and tap the side to release the sugar in an even layer over the shortcakes. Serve right away.

more ideas!

english scones

Follow the recipe for Strawberry Shortcakes but leave out the strawberries and whipped cream ingredients. In step 2, add 2 teaspoons grated orange or lemon zest and ½ cup dried currants, raisins, or dried cranberries to the dough before adding the cream. Cut out the dough and bake as directed. To serve, split the scones with a fork and serve with butter and jam.

blackberry shortcakes

Follow the recipe to make the shortcake rounds. Instead of topping them with strawberries, use 1 basket of blackberries. You can also make blackberry whipped cream instead of regular whipped cream: Mash another basket of blackberries with 1 tablespoon sugar. Put the fruit in a fine-mesh sieve and use a wooden spoon to push it through the sieve. Mix the berry mixture with 1 cup cold heavy cream and 1 teaspoon vanilla extract. Whip the mixture until soft peaks form.

peach shortcakes

Follow the recipe for Strawberry Shortcakes but replace the berries with 4 sliced and peeled peaches. To peel peaches, cut a shallow X in the bottom of each peach. Ask an adult to help you lower 2 peaches with a slotted spoon into a pan of boiling water. When the skins start to wrinkle, after 20–40 seconds, scoop the peaches out and immerse them in cold water. Repeat with the other 2 peaches. Starting at the X, peel each peach. Then halve, pit, and slice the peaches.

strawberry, blackberry, or peach shortcakes? you choose!

chocolate pudding

makes

6

servings

ingredients

sugar ¾ cup

cornstarch ⅓ cup

salt ¼ teaspoon

unsweetened chocolate 3 ounces

whole milk 4 cups

vanilla extract 1 teaspoon

whipped cream (page 25)
for serving

chocolate sprinkles for serving

tools

measuring cups & spoons

medium heatproof bowl

whisk

serrated knife & cutting board

medium saucepan

heatproof rubber spatula

ladle

1 prep the ingredients

✱ Before you start, be sure an adult is nearby to help.

✱ In the medium bowl, use the whisk to stir together the sugar, cornstarch, and salt. Set aside. Use the serrated knife to chop the chocolate into small bits.

2 melt the chocolate

✱ Put the milk and vanilla in the saucepan. Place over medium heat and warm until tiny bubbles appear around the edges of the pan. Add the chocolate and stir with the rubber spatula until the chocolate is melted, about 1 minute.

✱ Carefully ladle about one-fourth of the hot milk into the sugar mixture and whisk until everything is smooth.

3 mix it all together

✱ Add the remaining hot milk and whisk again until the mixture is smooth. Add this mixture back to the saucepan and place over medium heat.

✱ Stir the mixture with the rubber spatula until it begins to thicken. Use the spatula to scrape the bottom and corners of the pan to make sure those parts don't burn.

4 cook, cool & serve

✱ Cook the mixture until very thick, about 2 minutes. To test it, run your finger through the mixture on the spatula (let it cool a bit first!); it should leave a distinct trail.

✱ Ladle the pudding into bowls and let it cool for at least 30 minutes. Top with whipped cream and chocolate sprinkles.

baked delights

sweet lemon cupcakes

ingredients

lemons 2, washed

all-purpose flour 2¼ cups

baking powder 1½ teaspoons

salt ¾ teaspoon

poppy seeds 5 teaspoons

unsalted butter ¾ cup (1½ sticks),
at room temperature

granulated sugar 1½ cups

large eggs 2, at room temperature

whole milk ¾ cup

powdered sugar 2 cups

yellow and green decorating sugar

tools

measuring cups & spoons

two 12-cup muffin pans

24 cupcake liners

cutting board & sharp knife

box grater-shredder

small, medium & large bowls

whisk

electric mixer

rubber spatula

2 large spoons

thin bamboo skewer

oven mitts & cooling racks

citrus juicer

1 zest the lemons

✳ Before you start, be sure an adult is nearby to help.

✳ Position the oven racks in the upper and lower thirds of the oven. Preheat the oven to 325°F. Line the muffin pans with cupcake liners.

✳ Holding the lemons over the cutting board, rub them over the small holes of the grater. Use short strokes and turn the lemon as you work. Rub off only the colored part of the peel (the zest). Measure out 2 teaspoons zest. Reserve the lemons.

2 start the batter

✳ In the medium bowl, use the whisk to stir together the flour, baking powder, salt, and poppy seeds until evenly blended. Add the 2 teaspoons lemon zest to the flour mixture and whisk well.

✳ In the large bowl, using the electric mixer on medium speed, beat the butter until it is soft and fluffy.

✳ Turn off the mixer, sprinkle in the granulated sugar, and continue beating until pale.

✱ If you fill your muffin cups too full with batter, you'll end up with overblown cupcakes!

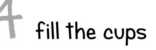

3 finish the batter

✱ One at a time, crack the eggs into the small bowl and check for shells. Add the eggs to the batter, one at a time, beating well after adding each one.

✱ Turn off the mixer and scrape down the sides of the bowl with the rubber spatula. Add half of the flour mixture and mix on low speed just until blended.

✱ Turn off the mixer and add the milk. Mix on low speed until smooth. Turn off the mixer and add the rest of the flour mixture. Mix just until blended.

4 fill the cups

✱ Scrape down the sides of the bowl with the rubber spatula. Then, using the two large spoons, one to scoop out the batter and the other to push it off the spoon, fill each muffin cup half full. Don't fill the muffin cups any higher than that.

✱ Wash the bowls and spoons.

✱ Fill them just the right amount and they'll have flat tops. Then, the icing won't flow over the sides and they'll be easier to decorate.

avoided!

5 bake the cupcakes

✳ Put the pans in the oven and bake until the edges of the cupcakes are pale golden brown and a thin skewer inserted into the center of a cupcake comes out clean (ask an adult to help!), 20–25 minutes.

✳ Ask an adult to help you remove the pans from the oven and put them on the cooling racks. Let the cupcakes cool in the pans for 10 minutes, then lift out the cakes, put them directly on the racks, and let cool completely, about 45 minutes.

6 make the icing

✳ Holding each zested lemon on its side on the cutting board, cut the lemons in half with the knife. Twist each lemon half over the cone of the juicer. Pick out and throw away any seeds. Measure out 3 tablespoons juice and put in the small bowl.

✳ In the medium bowl, whisk together the powdered sugar and a little of the lemon juice. Add some more lemon juice, but only enough to make the icing thick. It should slowly fall off the whisk.

7 ice & decorate

✳ Spoon some icing on top of each cupcake and use the back of the spoon in a circular motion to help spread it to the edges of the cupcake liner. Let the icing stand for a minute until it smooths out to make a flat surface.

✳ Right away, sprinkle the iced cupcakes with the colored sugar. Don't wait too long after pouring the icing, or it will harden and the sugar won't stick.

plum buckle

ingredients

all-purpose flour 1½ cups

baking powder 1 teaspoon

salt ¼ teaspoon

unsalted butter 1 cup (2 sticks),
at room temperature

sugar 1 cup

large eggs 2, at room temperature

large plums 6–8, pitted and
sliced into wedges ½ inch thick

cinnamon sugar 1 teaspoon
ground cinnamon mixed with
1 tablespoon sugar

tools

measuring cups & spoons

9-inch pie dish

cutting board

paring knife

medium & large bowls

whisk

electric mixer

rubber spatula

thin bamboo skewer

oven mitts & cooling rack

1 before you start

✳ Be sure an adult is nearby to help.
Position an oven rack in the center
of the oven. Preheat the oven to 350°F.

✳ Butter the pie dish well.

2 mix the ingredients

✳ In the medium bowl, use the whisk
to stir together the flour, baking powder,
and salt until evenly blended. Set aside.

✳ In the large bowl, using the electric
mixer on medium speed, beat the butter
until it is light and fluffy. Sprinkle in the
sugar and continue beating until pale.

✳ Turn off the mixer, scrape the bowl
with the rubber spatula, and add the eggs
one at a time, beating well after adding
each one.

3 finish the batter

✳ Beat in the flour mixture.

✳ Using the rubber spatula, scrape
the batter into the pie dish and spread
it out evenly.

4 top & bake

✳ Press the plum slices, close together
and skin side up, into the batter. Sprinkle
the plums with the cinnamon sugar.

✳ Bake for 45–50 minutes. To test if the
buckle is done, ask an adult to help you
pull out the oven rack and insert the skewer
into the center of the buckle. It should
come out clean. Wearing oven mitts, remove
the pan from the oven and place it on the
cooling rack. Let it cool completely before
cutting into wedges and serving.

golden layer cake

ingredients

all-purpose flour 3 cups

baking powder 2 teaspoons

salt ½ teaspoon

unsalted butter 1 cup (2 sticks), at room temperature

granulated sugar 2 cups

large eggs 4, at room temperature

buttermilk 1 cup

FROSTING & DECORATION

semisweet chocolate chips 1 cup

unsalted butter ¼ cup (½ stick)

sour cream ½ cup

vanilla extract 1 teaspoon

powdered sugar 2½ cups

chocolate syrup for making designs

tools

measuring cups & spoons

two 8-inch round cake pans

parchment paper, pencil & scissors

small, medium & large bowls

whisk & electric mixer

rubber spatula

thin bamboo skewer

oven mitts & cooling racks

table knife

saucepan & heatproof bowl

offset icing spatula

1 prepare the pans

* Before you start, be sure an adult is nearby to help.

* Position the oven racks so the cake layers can both bake close to the center of the oven. Preheat the oven to 350°F.

* Swab a small amount of butter on a paper towel and rub it evenly over the bottom and sides of the baking pans. Trace the bottoms of the cake pans onto the sheets of parchment paper and cut out the circles with the scissors. Use the parchment circles to line the pans.

2 start the batter

* In the medium bowl, use the whisk to stir together the flour, baking powder, and salt until evenly blended. Set aside.

* In the large bowl, using the electric mixer on medium speed, beat the butter until it is soft and fluffy.

* Turn off the mixer and sprinkle in the sugar. Continue beating until pale.

* Turn off the mixer and scrape down the sides of the bowl with the rubber spatula.

3 add the eggs

✳ Crack the eggs into the small bowl, check for shells, then whisk the eggs together. Add about half the beaten eggs to the batter and beat well on medium speed to incorporate them into the butter mixture.

✳ Turn off the mixer and add the rest of the eggs and beat on medium speed until incorporated.

✳ Turn off the mixer and scrape down the sides of the bowl with the rubber spatula.

4 alternate wet & dry

✳ Add about one-third of the flour mixture to the butter-egg mixture and mix on low speed just until blended.

✳ Turn off the mixer and pour in half of the buttermilk. Mix just until blended.

✳ Repeat, adding about one-third of the flour, the remaining buttermilk, and then the rest of the flour, mixing after each addition just until blended.

✳ Turn off the mixer and scrape down the sides of the bowl with the rubber spatula.

5 fill the pans & bake

✳ Use the rubber spatula to divide the batter evenly between the cake pans. Still using the rubber spatula, gently smooth the tops.

✳ Put the cake pans in the oven and bake until the cakes are golden brown and the skewer inserted into the centers of the cakes comes out clean (ask an adult to help!), 45–50 minutes.

6 cool the cakes

✳ Ask an adult to help you remove the cake pans from the oven and set them on cooling racks to cool for 20 minutes.

✳ Wash the spatula and mixer beaters.

✳ Run the table knife around the inside edge of each cake pan. Turn the pans over onto the cooling racks. Lift away the pans and let the cakes cool completely, upside down, on the racks, about 2 hours.

7 melt the chocolate

✳ Select a saucepan into which the heatproof bowl will fit snugly. Fill the pan one-third full of water, making sure the water doesn't reach the bottom of the bowl. Place the saucepan over medium heat.

✳ When the water is steaming, place the bowl on top of the saucepan and add the chocolate chips to the bowl.

✳ Heat, stirring with the rubber spatula, until the chocolate is melted and smooth. Remove the bowl from the saucepan and set aside. Remove the pan from the heat.

8 make the frosting

✳ Use the rubber spatula to stir the butter, sour cream, and vanilla into the melted chocolate. With the electric mixer on low speed, beat in the powdered sugar ½ cup at a time. When all the sugar has been added, increase the speed to high and beat until the frosting is smooth. Scrape down the sides of the bowl with the spatula and beat for one minute more.

✳ Frost, decorate, and slice the cake (turn to pages 44–45).

✳ Serve the cake right away, or cover it loosely with plastic wrap and refrigerate for up to 3 days.

how to frost a cake

frost the first layer 9

When the cake is cooled, remove the parchment from one layer and place the layer flat side up on a cake stand or plate. Using an offset spatula, spread half the frosting over the top, almost all the way to the edge, making it as even as possible. You don't need to go to the edge, because the weight of the top layer will push the frosting out more.

10 frost the second layer

Remove the parchment from the second cake layer and place it flat side down on top of the frosting. Try to line up the sides of the cakes. Spread the remaining frosting over the top of the cake, starting in the middle and working outward all the way to the edge.

decorate the top 11

Starting in the middle and working outward, drizzle a spiral of chocolate syrup on the top of the cake. Lightly drag a skewer through the frosting from the center outward to make a pattern. To serve, ask an adult to help you use a long, thin knife to cut the cake into 8 wedges.

use your imagination to create your own cake designs!

easy cheesy pie

ingredients

graham cracker squares 15

unsalted butter 4 tablespoons
(½ stick), melted

sugar 3 tablespoons

ground cinnamon ¼ teaspoon

lemon 1, scrubbed

cream cheese 2 packages
(8 ounces each), at room
temperature

sweetened condensed milk 1 can
(14 fluid ounces)

**raspberries, blackberries,
blueberries, or sliced strawberries**
for decorating (optional)

tools

measuring cups & spoons

can opener

heavy-duty lock-top plastic bag

rolling pin

small & medium bowls

wooden spoon

9-inch pie dish

oven mitts & cooling rack

cutting board & sharp knife

box grater-shredder

citrus juicer

electric mixer

rubber spatula

1 before you start

✳ Be sure an adult is nearby to help.

✳ Position an oven rack in the center
of the oven. Preheat the oven to 350°F.

2 make the crumbs

✳ Put the graham crackers in the lock-top
plastic bag and press out the air. Seal the
bag. Use the rolling pin to crush the graham
crackers into fine crumbs, hitting the crackers
softly or using a gentle back-and-forth
rolling motion.

✳ Measure out 1¼ cups of the crumbs.

3 mix the crust

✻ In the medium bowl, combine the graham cracker crumbs, melted butter, sugar, and cinnamon.

✻ Stir the mixture with the wooden spoon until the crumbs are well moistened and even in color.

4 shape & bake

✻ Using your fingertips, pat the crust mixture firmly into the pie dish, bringing it all the way up the sides of the dish.

✻ Put the pie dish in the oven and bake until the crust is firm, 6–7 minutes.

✻ Ask an adult to help you remove the pie dish from the oven and place it on the cooling rack. Let it cool completely, about 30 minutes. Meanwhile, continue with steps 5 & 6.

5 zest the lemon

✻ Holding the lemon over the cutting board, rub it over the small holes of the grater. Use short strokes and turn the lemon as you work. Rub off only the colored part of the peel (the zest). Measure out 1 teaspoon lemon zest and add it to the small bowl.

✻ Cut the lemon in half. Twist the lemon halves over the cone of the juicer to extract the juice. Pick out and throw away any seeds. Measure out 3 tablespoons lemon juice and add it to the small bowl.

6 make the filling

✳ Wash and dry the medium bowl. Put the cream cheese in the bowl and beat with the electric mixer on medium speed until the cheese is smooth, about 2 minutes. Turn off the mixer and add the sweetened condensed milk. Beat until smooth, about 1 minute.

✳ Turn off the mixer and scrape down the sides of the bowl with the rubber spatula.

✳ Add the lemon zest and juice and beat until the filling is smooth, about 30 seconds.

7 fill & chill

✳ Using the rubber spatula, scrape the filling into the baked and cooled pie crust. Use the spatula to spread the filling evenly in the crust and smooth the top.

✳ Put the pie the refrigerator until it is well chilled, about 3 hours.

8 decorate the pie

✳ If desired, top the pie with the berries in any pattern you like.

✳ Ask an adult to help you cut the pie into 8 wedges and serve.

chocolate galore

black bottom cupcakes

ingredients

FILLING

large egg 1, at room temperature

sugar 1/2 cup

cream cheese 1 package
(8 ounces), at room temperature

cold water 2 1/4 cups

vegetable oil 3/4 cup

vanilla extract 1 tablespoon

balsamic vinegar 5 teaspoons

all-purpose flour 3 1/2 cups

cocoa powder 3/4 cup

baking soda 2 teaspoons

sugar 2 1/4 cups

salt 1 teaspoon

semisweet chocolate chips 3/4 cup

tools

measuring cups & spoons

two 12-cup muffin pans

24 paper cupcake liners

medium & large bowls

electric mixer

pastry bag fitted with plain round tip

tall glass or mug

rubber spatula

whisk & wooden spoon

thin bamboo skewer

oven mitts & cooling racks

1 before you start

* Be sure an adult is nearby to help.

* Position the oven racks in the lower and upper thirds of the oven. Preheat the oven to 350°F.

* Line the muffin pans with the paper cupcake liners.

2 make the filling

* In the medium bowl, using the electric mixer on medium speed, beat the egg, sugar, and cream cheese until smooth, about 2 minutes.

* Prop up the pastry bag in a sturdy glass or mug with the bag's wide opening at the top. Fold the top of the pastry bag down over the glass. Using the rubber spatula, scrape the filling mixture into the pastry bag. Set the filled pastry bag aside.

3 mix the liquids

✳ In a large liquid measuring cup, combine the water, oil, vanilla extract, and balsamic vinegar. (There's no need to stir these. Just put them together in the cup.) Set aside.

4 make the batter

✳ In the large bowl, use the whisk to stir together the flour, cocoa powder, baking soda, sugar, and salt until evenly blended.

✳ Slowly pour the wet ingredients into the flour mixture, stirring with the wooden spoon until the batter is smooth.

why is there vinegar in my cupcake batter?

✳ Baking soda, the ingredient that makes these cupcakes rise, starts to work only when it comes in contact with an acidic ingredient. Some common types used in baking are lemon juice, buttermilk, and vinegar. Sweet balsamic vinegar, which has a flavor that goes well with the rich flavor of cocoa, is added to the batter here. It gives these cupcakes a deep, full flavor. Surprisingly, they won't taste anything like vinegar after the batter is baked.

5 pour in the batter

* The cupcake batter will be quite runny. If your bowl has a spout, you can pour the batter directly into the muffin cups. Otherwise, it will be easiest to pour the batter into the liquid measuring cup and use it to fill the cups. Fill each lined muffin cup three-quarters full. Don't fill them any fuller than that or there won't be anywhere for the filling to go when the batter rises!

6 add the filling

* Pick up the pastry bag. Plugging the tip with one hand, twist the top of the bag to close it. Using one hand to guide the tip and the other to squeeze the top of the bag, insert the tip into the center of one of the cupcakes. Gently squeeze a small amount of the cream cheese filling into the batter. You will see the chocolate batter rise as the filling fills the middle.

* Keeping in mind that you need to fill 24 cupcakes, squeeze a small amount into each one.

7 bake the cupcakes

* Sprinkle the top of each cupcake with the chocolate chips.

* Put the muffin pans in the oven and bake until a thin skewer inserted into the center of a cupcake comes out clean (ask an adult to help!), 26–28 minutes.

* Ask an adult to help you remove the pans from the oven and put them on the cooling racks. Let the cupcakes cool in the pans for 20 minutes, then lift out the cupcakes and put them directly on the racks. Let cool completely, about 30 minutes.

chocolate fondue

ingredients

strawberries 20

blackberries or raspberries 20

purchased pound cake one
8-by-4-inch loaf

large marshmallows 10

bananas 4

semisweet chocolate 8 ounces

heavy cream 1 cup

light corn syrup ½ cup

tools

measuring cups & spoons

colander

cutting board & paring knife

serrated knife

small saucepan

heatproof rubber spatula

fondue pot & small candle
for heating

fondue forks for serving

1 wash the berries

✱ Before you start, be sure an adult is
nearby to help.

✱ Put the berries in the colander in small
batches. Thoroughly rinse the berries under
cold running water, taking care not to crush
them. Place the rinsed berries in a single
layer on paper towels to air-dry before using.
(Or, you can pat them dry with the towels
if you are in a hurry.)

2 trim the berries

✱ Put the strawberries on the cutting board.
Using the paring knife, cut a thick slice from
the top of each berry to remove the stem.

✱ Pinch off the stems, if present, from the
blackberries or raspberries.

✱ Arrange all the berries in piles on a large
serving platter.

3 cut the pound cake

* Put the pound cake on the cutting board. Using the serrated knife, cut the loaf into 6 thick slices. Cut each slice into quarters to make 24 large cubes. Arrange the cake cubes on a serving platter.

* Arrange the marshmallows on a serving platter.

4 cut the bananas

* Wipe the cutting board. Peel the bananas and put them on the board. Using the paring knife, cut each banana crosswise into 5 or more thick chunks. Arrange the banana chunks on the serving platter.

5 chop the chocolate

* Wipe the cutting board and wash and dry the serrated knife.

* Put the chocolate on the cutting board and chop the chocolate into small bits. Try to make the bits as even as possible so they will melt at the same time.

6 melt the chocolate

✳ Put the chocolate, cream, and corn syrup in the small saucepan.

✳ Place the saucepan over low heat and warm until tiny bubbles appear in the cream around the edges of the pan. Stir the mixture occasionally with the rubber spatula until the chocolate is melted and smooth, 10–12 minutes. Don't let the chocolate get too hot. Remove the saucepan from the heat.

7 fill the fondue pot

✳ Using the rubber spatula, carefully scrape the chocolate mixture into the fondue pot.

✳ Ask an adult to help you place the fondue pot on the table and light the candle beneath it.

8 serve the fondue

✳ Give each diner a small plate and a fondue fork and pass the platter of fruit, marshmallows, and cake. Take turns skewering fruit or cake and dipping it in the warm chocolate fondue. Eat right away! (The chocolate is meant to be kept warm, not hot. If the temperature gets too hot, blow out the candle and continue to enjoy your treat.)

chocolate truffles

ingredients

unsalted butter ¼ cup (½ stick)

semisweet chocolate 8 ounces

heavy cream ¼ cup

vanilla extract ¼ teaspoon

powdered sugar or **unsweetened cocoa powder** ¼ cup

tools

measuring cups & spoons

cutting board & table knife

serrated knife

small saucepan

oven mitts

heatproof rubber spatula

2 shallow bowls

plastic wrap

small melon baller

1 chop the ingredients

✳ Before you start, be sure an adult is nearby to help.

✳ Put the butter on the cutting board. Using the table knife, cut the butter into small chunks. Set aside.

✳ Put the chocolate on the cutting board. Using the serrated knife, chop the chocolate into small, even bits. Set aside.

2 warm the cream

✳ Add the cream to the saucepan. Place over medium heat and warm until tiny bubbles appear in the cream around the edges of the pan. Turn off the heat.

3 melt the chocolate

✳ Add the butter and chocolate to the saucepan and stir with the rubber spatula until everything is melted and the mixture is very smooth.

✳ If the chocolate doesn't seem to be melting, turn on the heat to medium and warm for about 20 seconds. Turn off the heat and stir again.

✳ Repeat the heating and stirring process, if necessary, until the mixture is smooth. Don't let the mixture get too hot.

4 chill the mixture

✳ Let the mixture cool to the touch, about 15 minutes. Using the rubber spatula, stir in the vanilla extract. Scrape the mixture into one of the shallow bowls.

✳ Cover the chocolate mixture with plastic wrap and refrigerate until it is solid, at least 4 hours or overnight.

5 scoop the truffles

✳ Using the melon baller, scoop the chocolate mixture to make rough balls the size of a gumball. (The chocolate will be rather firm, so you may want to ask an adult to help with the scooping.) Place each scoop of truffle mixture onto a cool work surface.

problem?

✳ If the truffles are becoming soft and messy as you shape them, your hands are too warm.

✳ To fix this, dip your hands into ice water, then dry them thoroughly. You can also refrigerate the truffles to firm them up before coating.

solved!

6 shape the truffles

✳ Put the powdered sugar or the cocoa in the other shallow bowl. (The powdered sugar will give the truffles an extra layer of sweetness. The cocoa will make the truffles intensely chocolatey.)

✳ Working with 1 truffle scoop at a time, use the palms of your hands to roll it into a smooth, round ball.

✳ After rolling, put the balls in the bowl with the coating of your choice.

7 coat the truffles

✳ Roll each truffle in the powdered sugar or cocoa powder until it is completely coated, then put in a serving dish.

✳ Cover and store the truffles in the refrigerator until you are ready to eat them. (You can even freeze the truffles for up to 3 months.)

more ideas!

sprinkle-coated truffles

Follow the recipe for Chocolate Truffles but leave out the powdered sugar or cocoa powder coating. In step 7, roll the truffles in multicolored or chocolate sprinkles instead.

nutty truffles

Follow the recipe for Chocolate Truffles but leave out the powdered sugar or cocoa powder coating. In step 4, add ¾ teaspoon almond extract along with the vanilla. In step 7, roll the truffles in ¼ cup natural almonds that have been toasted and finely chopped (page 94).

flavored truffles

It's simple to change the flavor of the truffles. Follow the recipe for Chocolate Truffles. For Zesty Orange Truffles, in step 4, add 1 teaspoon orange oil along with the vanilla. For Mellow Mocha Truffles, add 1 tablespoon coffee powder dissolved in 1 teaspoon water along with the vanilla. For Cool Mint Truffles, add 1 teaspoon mint or peppermint extract along with the vanilla. Continue with the recipe as directed.

you can coat truffles with almost anything you like!

rocky road fudge

ingredients

vegetable oil ½ teaspoon
mini marshmallows 3½ cups
coarsely chopped walnuts 2 cups
semisweet chocolate chips 2 cups
sweetened condensed milk 1 can
(14 fluid ounces)
vanilla extract 1 teaspoon

tools

measuring cups & spoons
sharp knife & cutting board
can opener
8-inch square baking pan
aluminum foil
medium microwave-safe bowl
heatproof rubber spatula
plastic wrap

1 before you start

✳ Be sure an adult is nearby to help.

✳ Line the baking pan with the aluminum foil, gently pressing the foil into the corners and letting the foil hang over the sides.

✳ Soak a paper towel with the vegetable oil and use it to rub over the foil.

✳ Set aside ½ cup walnuts and ½ cup mini marshmallows.

2 melt the chocolate

✳ Put the chocolate chips and condensed milk in the bowl and microwave on high for 1 minute. Stir with the rubber spatula. If the chips aren't melted, return to the microwave 1 or 2 times for 30 seconds each, stirring after each time, just until the chocolate is melted. Don't let the chocolate get too hot.

3 mix the ingredients

✳ Using the rubber spatula, gently stir the vanilla extract, 3 cups of the marshmallows, and 1½ cups of the walnuts into the chocolate mixture.

✳ Using the spatula, scrape the chocolate mixture into the prepared baking pan. Spread it out evenly and smooth the top.

4 decorate & chill

✳ Sprinkle the fudge with the reserved marshmallows and walnuts and gently press them into the surface. Cover the pan with plastic wrap and refrigerate until firm, at least 30 minutes.

✳ Lift the foil to remove the fudge from the pan and peel away the foil. Cut the fudge into 16 pieces.

raid the cookie jar

double-chocolate cookies

makes
24
cookies

ingredients

semisweet bar chocolate 8 ounces

unsalted butter 1/3 cup

all-purpose flour 1/3 cup

baking powder 1/4 teaspoon

salt 1/4 teaspoon

sugar 1 cup

large eggs 2, at room temperature

semisweet chocolate chips 1 cup

tools

measuring cups & spoons

cutting board & serrated knife

table knife

small saucepan

heatproof rubber spatula

medium & large mixing bowls

whisk

wooden spoon

2 cookie sheets

parchment paper

oven mitts & cooling racks

metal spatula

1 chop the ingredients

✳ Before you start, be sure an adult is nearby to help.

✳ Put the bar chocolate on the cutting board. Use the serrated knife to chop the chocolate into small, even bits.

✳ Switch to the table knife and cut the butter into chunks.

2 melt the chocolate

✳ In the saucepan, combine the chocolate and butter.

✳ Place the saucepan over medium-low heat and warm until the butter melts. Don't let the chocolate get too hot. Remove the pan from the heat and stir the mixture with the rubber spatula until the chocolate is melted and the mixture is smooth.

raid the cookie jar **71**

3 mix the dough

* In the medium bowl, use the whisk to stir together the flour, baking powder, and salt until evenly blended.

* In the large bowl, using the wooden spoon, stir together the sugar and eggs until well blended. Add the chocolate mixture and stir until blended.

* Add half the flour mixture and stir until blended. Add the rest of the flour mixture and stir until blended.

* Stir in the chocolate chips.

4 let the dough stand

* Let the dough stand until it has firmed up enough to be scooped, about 1 hour.

* Position the oven rack in the middle of the oven. Preheat the oven to 350°F.

* Line the cookie sheets with the parchment paper.

5 scoop the dough

* Using a measuring tablespoon, scoop up a rounded spoonful of dough and then use your finger to push the dough onto one of the prepared cookie sheets.

* Fill both cookie sheets with the dough, placing the lumps of dough 2 inches apart so that the cookies have room to spread as they bake. You should be able to fit 12 cookies on each cookie sheet.

6 flatten the cookies

✱ With wet fingers, gently press each cookie in the middle a little bit. This will flatten the cookies and help them bake more evenly.

7 bake the cookies

✱ When the first cookie sheet is full, put it in the oven and bake the cookies until the sides are firm and the centers are soft to the touch, about 15 minutes. Do not overbake, or your cookies will be dry.

8 let the cookies cool

✱ Ask an adult to help you remove the cookie sheet from the oven and set it on a cooling rack for 10 minutes.

✱ Move the cookies directly onto the rack with the metal spatula and let them cool completely before eating.

✱ As the first batch of cookies is cooling, bake the rest of the cookies.

thumbprint cookies

ingredients

orange 1, washed

all-purpose flour 2 cups

baking powder ½ teaspoon

salt ¼ teaspoon

unsalted butter 1 cup (2 sticks), at room temperature

sugar ½ cup

vanilla extract ¾ teaspoon

almond extract ¼ teaspoon

raspberry jam 1–2 tablespoons

apricot jam 1–2 tablespoons

blackberry jam 1–2 tablespoons

tools

measuring cups & spoons

2 cookie sheets

parchment paper

cutting board

box grater-shredder

medium & large bowls

whisk

electric mixer

rubber spatula

oven mitts

cooling racks

metal spatula

1 before you start

* Be sure an adult is nearby to help.

* Position the oven racks in the lower and upper thirds of the oven. Preheat the oven to 350°F.

* Line the cookie sheets with the parchment paper.

2 zest the orange

* Holding the orange over the cutting board, rub it over the small grating holes of the box grater-shredder. Use short strokes and turn the orange as you work. Rub off only the colored part of the peel (the zest), avoiding the bitter white pith underneath. Measure out 1 teaspoon zest and set aside.

3 mix the dry things

✳ In the medium bowl, use the whisk to stir together the flour, baking powder, and salt until evenly blended. Set aside.

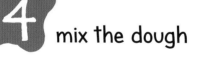

4 mix the dough

✳ In the large bowl, using the electric mixer on medium speed, beat the butter until it is soft and fluffy.

✳ Turn off the mixer and sprinkle in the sugar. Continue beating until pale. Turn off the mixer and scrape down the bowl with the rubber spatula.

✳ Add the orange zest, vanilla extract, and almond extract and beat until blended.

✳ Turn off the mixer and add half the flour mixture. Mix on low just until blended. Add the remaining flour and mix until blended.

5 scoop the dough

✳ Using a measuring tablespoon, scoop up a rounded spoonful of dough and then use your finger to push the dough onto one of the prepared cookie sheets. Fill both cookie sheets with the dough, placing the lumps of dough 2 inches apart so that the cookies have room to spread as they bake. You should be able to fit 12 cookies on each cookie sheet.

6 make the thumbprints

✳ Dip your thumb in a little bit of flour and use it to make a dent in each ball of dough. (This process of making dents with your thumb is how the cookies get their name.)

7 fill & bake

✳ Fill each dent with a small amount of jam, scooping the jam with a teaspoon and pushing off just what you need with your finger. You can vary the types of jam you use to make different flavors of cookies.

✳ When the cookie sheets are full, put them in the oven and bake until the cookies are lightly browned, about 18 minutes.

8 let cool & serve

✳ Ask an adult to help you remove the cookie sheets from the oven and set them on the cooling racks for 10 minutes.

✳ Move the cookies directly onto the racks with the metal spatula and let them cool completely before eating.

✳ Line 1 cookie sheet with a new sheet of parchment and repeat steps 5–8 to bake and cool the rest of the cookies.

more ideas!

fruit thumbprints

Follow the recipe for Thumbprint Cookies but leave out the jams. In step 7, after you have made a dent in each cookie, press half a dried apricot into each dent (you'll need 32 dried apricot halves in all). Continue with the recipe as directed to bake the cookies.

chocolate thumbprints

Follow the recipe for Thumbprint Cookies but leave out the jams. In step 7, after you have made a dent in each cookie, press a chocolate kiss into each dent (you'll need 32 chocolate kisses in all). Continue with the recipe as directed to bake the cookies.

sprinkle balls

Follow the recipe for Thumbprint Cookies but leave out the jams. Also omit step 6, which calls for making a dent in each cookie. Instead, in step 5, roll each scoop of dough gently between your palms to make a ball and then press one side into a bowl of multicolored sprinkles or decorating sugar. Place the cookies, sprinkle side up, on the cookie sheet and continue with the recipe as directed to bake the cookies.

you can make 4 different cookies from the same dough!

peanut butter bars

ingredients

all-purpose flour 1 cup

rolled oats 1 cup

baking soda ½ teaspoon

salt ¼ teaspoon

butter ½ cup (1 stick), at room temperature

brown sugar 1 cup, firmly packed

creamy or chunky peanut butter ½ cup

large egg 1, at room temperature

vanilla extract 1 teaspoon

powdered sugar for dusting

tools

measuring cups & spoons

8-inch square baking pan

parchment paper

medium & large bowls

whisk

electric mixer

rubber spatula

oven mitts & cooling rack

small fine-mesh sieve

cutting board & sharp knife

1 before you start

✳ Be sure an adult is nearby to help. Position an oven rack in the center of the oven. Preheat the oven to 350°F. Grease the baking pan with butter, then line it with parchment paper, letting it hang over 2 sides.

2 start the batter

✳ In the medium bowl, use the whisk to stir together the flour, oats, baking soda, and salt until well blended. Set aside.

✳ In the large bowl, using the electric mixer on medium speed, beat together the butter, brown sugar, and peanut butter until creamy, about 3 minutes.

✳ Turn off the mixer and scrape down the sides of the bowl with the rubber spatula.

3 finish the batter

✳ Add the egg and vanilla and beat well.

✳ Turn off the mixer and add the flour-oat mixture. Mix on low speed just until blended.

4 bake & cool

✳ Using the rubber spatula, scrape the batter into the pan and spread it evenly.

✳ Place the baking pan in the oven and bake until the top of the cookie is golden and looks firm, 25–30 minutes.

✳ Ask an adult to help you remove the baking pan from the oven and set it on the cooling rack. Let cool completely. Lift the cookie from the pan, dust it with powdered sugar, and cut it into 1-by-4-inch bars.

ice cream sandwiches

ingredients

semisweet chocolate chips 1 cup

unsalted butter ½ cup (1 stick)

light corn syrup ¼ cup

sugar ⅓ cup

large egg 1, at room temperature

vanilla extract 1 teaspoon

all-purpose flour 1 cup

baking soda ½ teaspoon

salt ¼ teaspoon

ice cream 1 quart

tools

measuring cups & spoons

2 cookie sheets

parchment paper

small saucepan

heatproof rubber spatula

large & medium bowls

wooden spoon

whisk

oven mitts & cooling racks

metal spatula

ice cream scoop

plastic wrap & lock-top plastic
bag (optional)

1 before you start

✳ Be sure an adult is nearby to help.

✳ Position the oven racks in the upper
and lower thirds of the oven. Preheat the
oven to 350°F.

✳ Line the cookie sheets with the
parchment paper.

2 melt the chocolate

✳ In the saucepan, combine the chocolate
chips, butter, and corn syrup. Place over
medium-low heat and warm until the butter
melts. Don't let the chocolate get too hot.
Remove from the heat and stir with the
rubber spatula until the chocolate is melted
and the mixture is smooth. Scrape into the
large bowl and let cool.

✳ Add the sugar to the bowl and stir well
with the wooden spoon. Stir in the egg and
vanilla until blended. Scrape down the sides
of the bowl with the rubber spatula.

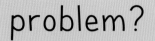

✳ If you put your cookies too close together on the baking sheet, they will meld together as they bake.

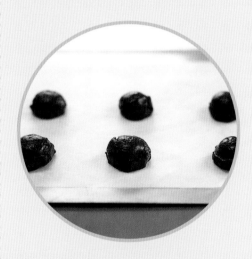

✳ Be sure the dough balls are far enough apart on the cookie sheet to account for their spreading, usually 2–4 inches apart.

3 mix the ingredients

✳ In the medium bowl, use the whisk to stir together the flour, baking soda, and salt until evenly blended.

✳ Add half of the flour mixture to the chocolate mixture and stir with the wooden spoon until blended.

✳ Add the rest of the flour mixture and stir until blended.

4 shape the cookies

✳ Using a measuring tablespoon, scoop up rounded spoonfuls of dough and place them 4 inches apart on the prepared cookie sheets so that they have room to spread as they bake.

✳ With your fingers, pat the lumps of dough to make them as round as possible so that they will spread into neat circles. You should be able to fit 9 cookies on each cookie sheet.

avoided!

5 bake & let cool

✳ When both cookie sheets are full, put them in the oven and bake the cookies until they have puffed and then begun to sink, 10–12 minutes. Do not overbake them, or they will be hard and brittle.

✳ Ask an adult to help you remove the cookie sheets from the oven and set them on the cooling racks for 15 minutes.

✳ Move the cookies directly onto the racks with the metal spatula and let them cool. Line the sheets with new parchment and bake the rest of the cookies.

6 scoop the ice cream

✳ Turn the cookies over on the rack so that the round side is facing down.

✳ Dip an ice cream scoop into hot water and warm briefly. Pull the scoop across the ice cream to form a rounded ball. Release the ball onto a cookie. Repeat until you have topped half of the cookies with ice cream.

7 make the sandwiches

✳ Place the remaining cookies, flat side down, on top of the ice cream.

✳ One at a time, pick up the ice cream sandwiches. Press the top cookies down to push the ice cream evenly to the edges of the cookies.

✳ Serve the sandwiches right away. Or if you are serving them later, wrap each sandwich individually in plastic wrap and place them together in a lock-top freezer bag. Freeze until ready to serve.

frozen wonders

89

strawberry ice cream

93

ice cream sundaes

99

truffle-mint ice cream cake

102

watermelon ice pops

strawberry ice cream

ingredients

fresh strawberries 2 baskets
(4 cups)

sour cream (not reduced fat)
2 cups

heavy cream 1 cup

sugar 1 cup

vanilla extract 1 teaspoon

salt 1 pinch

ice and rock salt if needed
for the ice cream maker

tools

measuring cups & spoons

ice cream maker

cutting board & paring knife

blender

rubber spatula

freezerproof storage container

ice cream scoop

1 before you start

✳ Be sure an adult is nearby to help.

✳ Read the instructions for your ice cream
maker, so you will know how it works.

✳ If your ice cream maker has a canister
that needs to be frozen, put it in the freezer
to chill at least 8 hours before you plan to
make the ice cream.

2 prepare the berries

✳ Put the strawberries on the cutting
board. Using the paring knife, cut a thick
slice from the top of each berry to remove
the green stem.

✳ Using the paring knife, cut the berries
into small pieces.

3 blend the ingredients

* In the blender container, combine the strawberries, sour cream, heavy cream, sugar, vanilla, and salt. (The salt helps intensify the berry flavor.)

* Cover the blender with the lid and hold the lid down while you blend on high speed until the mixture is smooth. You may need to stop the blender from time to time and scrape down the sides with the rubber spatula to get everything evenly blended.

4 get ready to freeze

* Pour the berry mixture into the chilled canister of your ice cream maker. Use the spatula to scrape out every last bit.

* Attach the hand crank if your machine has one. Fill the bucket with ice and sprinkle with rock salt if your ice cream maker needs it.

5 freeze the ice cream

* Freeze the berry mixture according to the manufacturer's directions. Some ice cream makers require you to crank the handle of the machine the entire time, while other machines do all the work for you.

why is ice cream so soft if it's frozen?

✱ Liquids usually turn hard as ice when frozen, but ice cream stays smooth and soft. The secret lies in constantly stirring the cream as it freezes. When a dense liquid like cream freezes, ice crystals form and grow in it. But if the crystals are constantly disturbed, they stay small and separate and the liquid doesn't solidify into a rock-solid hard block of ice.

6 ripen the ice cream

✱ Using the rubber spatula, scoop the ice cream into a freezerproof storage container with a lid and place it in the freezer to get firm (or "ripen") for 4 hours. (The ice cream can be eaten before this, but ripening it will give it a better texture and keep it from melting too quickly in your bowl.)

7 scoop & serve

✱ The ice cream is ready when it is firm and scoopable, but not overly soft.

✱ Dip an ice cream scoop into hot water and warm briefly. Pull the scoop across the ice cream to form a ball. Release the ball into the bowl, repeat to add more balls, if you like, and serve right away.

ice cream sundaes

ingredients

FUDGE SAUCE

semisweet chocolate chips 1 cup

unsalted butter ¼ cup (½ stick),
cut into pieces

whole milk ⅓ cup

powdered sugar ½ cup

vanilla extract 1 teaspoon

strawberries ½ cup

granulated sugar 1–2 teaspoons
plus 1 tablespoon

whole almonds 1 cup (optional)

favorite ice cream 1 pint

whipped cream (page 25)

tools

measuring cups & spoons

small saucepan

whisk

cutting board & paring knife

rimmed baking sheet

oven mitts

plate

sharp knife

small bowl

electric mixer

ice cream scoop

1 make the fudge sauce

✶ Before you start, be sure an adult is
nearby to help.

✶ Position the oven rack in the middle
of the oven. Preheat the oven to 325°F.

✶ In the small saucepan, combine the
chocolate chips, butter, milk, powdered
sugar, and vanilla extract.

✶ Place on the stove top over low heat.
Stir constantly with the whisk until the
chips are melted and the mixture is smooth.
Let the fudge sauce cool for 15 minutes.

2 trim the berries

✶ Put the strawberries on the cutting
board. Using the paring knife, cut a
thick slice from the top of each berry
to remove the stem.

✴ It's easy to burn nuts when you're toasting them. And burnt nuts taste terrible!

✴ Keep a close eye on the nuts when they're in the oven. Slide them off the hot pan as soon as they are browned and fragrant.

avoided!

3 chop the berries

✴ Using the paring knife, cut the berries into small pieces and put the pieces in the bowl. Sprinkle with the 1–2 teaspoons sugar (the amount depends on how sweet the berries are) and let stand for at least 10 minutes before using.

4 toast the almonds

✴ Spread the almonds in a single layer on the baking sheet. Place the baking sheet in the oven and toast the almonds, gently shaking the baking sheet occasionally (wear oven mitts!), until they are fragrant and lightly browned, about 12 minutes.

✴ Ask an adult to help you remove the pan from the oven and pour the almonds onto the plate. Let cool completely.

✴ Using the cutting board and sharp knife, chop the cooled almonds into small pieces. Set aside.

5 build one sundae

✳ In the bottom of a sundae glass or serving dish, spoon some of the still-warm fudge sauce.

✳ Dip the ice cream scoop into hot water and warm briefly. Pull the scoop across the ice cream to form a ball. Release the ball into the dish.

✳ Repeat to add a second scoop of ice cream and drizzle with more fudge sauce.

6 decorate the sundae

✳ Add a spoonful of chopped strawberries to the top of the sundae. Top with a swirl of whipped cream, then some chopped toasted almonds.

7 make more sundaes

✳ Repeat steps 5 & 6 to make 3 more sundaes. Serve them right away!

more ideas!

black & tan sundae

Follow the recipe for Ice Cream Sundaes but use chocolate ice cream and leave out the strawberries. In step 5, drizzle the ice cream with a little less fudge sauce. In step 6, drizzle the whipped cream with a little store-bought caramel sauce before adding the almonds.

chocolate brownie sundae

Swirl fudge sauce in the bottom of 4 bowls. Add 2 scoops of ice cream to each bowl. Arrange 1 brownie, cut into pieces, on top of each portion of ice cream and drizzle with the fudge sauce.

deluxe banana split

Swirl fudge sauce in the bottom of a large, flat sundae dish. Slice a banana lengthwise and place it on top of the sauce. Top the banana with 1 scoop each chocolate, vanilla, and strawberry ice cream. Drizzle fudge sauce on the chocolate ice cream, caramel sauce on the vanilla, and the chopped strawberries on the strawberry. Place a dollop of whipped cream in the middle, and sprinkle the whole thing with almonds. Serve with 2 spoons!

an extra-large banana split is enough for both you and a friend!

truffle-mint ice cream cake

ingredients

semisweet or bittersweet bar chocolate 8 ounces

heavy cream ¾ cup

mint extract 1 teaspoon

candy cane 1 stick or **peppermint candies** 4 or 5

powdered sugar ½ cup

peppermint or vanilla ice cream 2 quarts, softened

tools

measuring cups & spoons

cutting board & serrated knife

small saucepan

large wooden spoon

small heatproof bowl

plastic wrap

freezerproof loaf-shaped dish, 5 by 9 inches

lock-top plastic bag

rimmed baking sheet

melon baller

ice cream paddle (optional)

fork

long, thin knife for slicing

tall glass

1 melt the chocolate

✳ Before you start, be sure an adult is nearby to help. Put the chocolate on the cutting board and use the serrated knife to chop it into small, even bits.

✳ Add the cream to the saucepan. Place over medium heat and warm until tiny bubbles appear in the cream around the edges of the pan. Remove from the heat.

✳ Sprinkle the chopped chocolate into the hot cream and stir gently with the wooden spoon until the chocolate is melted. Stir in the mint extract.

2 chill the mixture

✳ Pour the chocolate mixture into the bowl and let it cool to room temperature. Then cover the bowl with plastic wrap and refrigerate until the mixture is firm, 2–3 hours or overnight.

✳ Put the loaf dish in the freezer to chill.

✳ Meanwhile, put the candy in the lock-top plastic bag, press out the air, and seal it. Using the wooden spoon, strike the candy firmly to break it into small bits. Set aside.

3 shape the truffles

✳ Spread the powdered sugar on the rimmed baking sheet. Remove the chocolate mixture from the refrigerator. With the melon baller, scoop out 16 balls, placing each ball on the baking sheet. These are the truffles.

✳ Put the remaining chocolate mixture back into the refrigerator until you need it.

✳ Gently roll the truffles in the powdered sugar to make them round and to give them a protective coating so that they will stay distinct and separate in your ice cream cake. Place the baking sheet in the freezer while you do the next step.

4 start layering

✳ Scoop about one-third of the ice cream into the bottom of the loaf dish to make a thick layer. Pack it as flat as possible with the ice cream paddle or wooden spoon.

5 arrange the truffles

✳ Gently press 8 truffles into the ice cream layer in a random pattern. You don't want to press them all the way to the bottom of the loaf dish.

6 fill in the layers

✳ Cover the truffles with another third of the ice cream, gently pressing the ice cream between them with the paddle.

✳ Press the remaining truffles into the ice cream, again in a random pattern.

✳ Cover the second layer of truffles with the remaining ice cream, filling in the gaps in between the truffles. Cover the loaf dish with plastic wrap and put it in the freezer until firm, 4–6 hours.

7 unmold the cake

✳ Ask an adult to help you run the outside of the loaf dish under hot tap water until you notice the ice cream melting slightly around the edges.

✳ Immediately turn the loaf dish over onto a flat serving platter. If the ice cream loaf does not drop out, briefly run it under hot water and try again.

✳ Put the serving plate with the ice cream cake back in the freezer.

8 decorate & serve

✳ Place the bowl with the chocolate in a dish filled with an inch or two of hot tap water and warm gently, stirring with the wooden spoon until the mixture is fluid.

✳ Remove the cake from the freezer. Dip the tines of the fork into the chocolate mixture and use it to drizzle chocolate all over the top of the cake. Sprinkle the cake with the peppermint candy pieces and return the cake to the freezer until serving.

✳ To serve each slice, dip the thin knife into a tall glass of hot water, wipe it clean, then use it to cut the ice cream cake into 1-inch slices. Serve right away.

watermelon ice pops

ingredients

watermelon chunks 4½ cups
sugar ½ cup
salt 1 pinch

tools

measuring cups & spoons
cutting board & paring knife
blender
8 frozen fruit pop molds
with sticks

1 seed the watermelon

✳ Before you start, be sure an adult is nearby to help.

✳ Put the watermelon chunks on the cutting board. If you see any black seeds in your watermelon chunks, use the point of the paring knife to carefully poke them out.

2 prepare to purée

✳ In the blender container, combine the watermelon chunks, sugar, and salt. (Salt might seem like a strange ingredient to add to a dessert, but it actually helps make the flavor of the watermelon more intense.)

3 blend the mixture

✳ Cover the blender with the lid and hold it down while you blend on high speed until the mixture is liquid (some small chunks of melon are okay).

4 freeze the pops

✳ Pour the mixture into a glass measuring cup with a spout, then divide the mixture evenly among the molds. Insert the sticks.

✳ Freeze the ice pops for at least 8 hours or overnight.

✳ Run the molds under warm water for 30 seconds to release the pops. Eat the pops right away!

favorite beverages

chocolate milk shake

ingredients

cold whole milk ¾ cup
chocolate ice cream as needed
chocolate syrup 2 tablespoons
whipped cream (page 25) (optional)

tools

measuring cups & spoons
blender
ice cream scoop
tall glass
long spoon or straw

1 blend the ingredients

✹ Before you start, be sure an adult is nearby to help.

✹ Add the milk to the blender.

✹ Dip the ice cream scoop into hot water and warm briefly. Pull the scoop across the ice cream to form a ball. Add the ball to the blender. Repeat to form a second scoop and add it to the blender.

✹ Cover the blender with the lid and hold it down while you blend on high speed until the mixture is smooth.

2 decorate & serve

✹ Drizzle a little chocolate syrup around the inside of a tall glass.

✹ Pour the shake into the glass.

✹ Top the milk shake with a dollop of whipped cream, if you like. Serve it right away with the long spoon or straw.

more ideas!

creamy orange frappé

Add 1 cup cold fresh orange juice to the blender container. Next, add 2 scoops of vanilla ice cream and 1 teaspoon vanilla extract. Blend on high speed until the mixture is smooth, then pour into a glass and serve.

malted milk shake

Add ¾ cup cold milk to the blender container. Next, add 2 scoops of vanilla or chocolate ice cream and 2–3 tablespoons malted milk powder, depending on how "malty" you like your shake. Blend on high speed until the mixture is smooth, then pour into a glass and serve.

fresh strawberry milk shake

Add ¾ cup cold milk to the blender container. Next, add 2 scoops of strawberry or vanilla ice cream and 1 cup sliced fresh strawberries. Blend on high speed until the mixture is smooth, then pour into a glass and serve.

to make more shakes, just double or triple the ingredients!

fresh lemonade

ingredients

large lemons 8 or 9
sugar 1 cup
cold water 5 cups
ice (optional)

tools

measuring cups & spoons
cutting board & sharp knife
citrus juicer
widemouthed pitcher
wooden spoon

1 juice the lemons

✱ Before you start, be sure an adult is nearby to help.

✱ Holding each lemon on its side on the cutting board, cut the lemons in half with the knife. Twist each lemon half over the cone of the juicer. Pick out and throw away any seeds. Measure out 1 cup lemon juice and pour it into the pitcher.

2 sweeten the juice

✱ Add the sugar to the lemon juice and, using the wooden spoon, stir until the sugar is dissolved. This will take a couple of minutes, so keep stirring. Add the water. Put the lemonade in the refrigerator for at least 30 minutes to chill before serving it. If you like, pour it over ice.

more ideas!

mint lemonade

Follow the recipe for Fresh Lemonade but add 10 sprigs washed and dried fresh mint. In a medium bowl, use the back of a spoon to crush the mint with the sugar. Let the mixture stand for 10 minutes. Add the lemon juice and stir until the sugar is dissolved. Strain the lemon mixture through a sieve into the pitcher, then add the water. Serve chilled.

ginger limeade

Follow the recipe for Fresh Lemonade but replace the lemons with 8 or 9 limes. Juice them as described in step 1. Peel a 2-inch chunk of fresh ginger with a vegetable peeler and cut it into thin slices. In a bowl, use the back of a spoon to crush the ginger with the sugar. Let the mixture stand for 10 minutes. Add the lime juice and stir until the sugar is dissolved. Strain through a sieve into the pitcher, then add the water. Serve chilled.

raspberry lemonade

Follow the recipe for Fresh Lemonade but add
1 cup rinsed and drained fresh raspberries.
In a medium bowl, use the back of a spoon to
crush the raspberries with the sugar. Let the
mixture stand for 10 minutes. Add the lemon
juice and stir until the sugar is dissolved.
Strain through a sieve into the pitcher, then
add the water. Serve chilled.

what's the secret to the best pink lemonade? fresh raspberries!

hot mulled cider

ingredients

orange 1, washed

apple juice or cranberry juice cocktail 4 cups (1 quart)

cinnamon sticks 2

whole cloves 4

tools

measuring cups & spoons

cutting board & sharp knife

medium saucepan

4 mugs

ladle

1 slice the orange

✳ Before you start, be sure an adult is nearby to help.

✳ Put the orange on the cutting board and use the knife to slice it crosswise to make 8 thick slices.

2 combine ingredients

✳ Choose whether you want apple juice or cranberry juice cocktail for your hot drink. (Apple juice is traditional but cranberry juice is a good choice during the holiday season.)

✳ Combine your juice of choice, the cinnamon sticks, and the cloves in the saucepan.

3 warm the mixture

✳ Place the saucepan over medium heat and warm the juice until tiny bubbles appear around the edges of the pan. Simmer gently for 20 minutes, reducing the heat as needed to keep the juice from boiling. Remove the pan from the heat.

4 serve the cider

✳ Place 1 orange slice in each mug. Ask an adult to help you ladle the hot cider over the orange slices.

✳ Decorate the edge of each mug with a second orange slice. First cut a slit into the center of the orange slice and then place it over the rim of the mug.

✳ Serve right away.

ice cream soda

ingredients

vanilla syrup 2 tablespoons
vanilla ice cream as needed
seltzer water or club soda ¾ cup

FOR SERVING (OPTIONAL)
whipped cream (page 25)
maraschino cherry

tools

measuring cups & spoons
tall glass
ice cream scoop
straw or long spoon

1 start with the syrup

✳ Before you start, be sure an adult is nearby to help.

✳ Drizzle the vanilla syrup into the bottom of the glass.

2 add the ice cream

✳ Dip the ice cream scoop into hot water and warm briefly. Pull the scoop across the ice cream to form a ball. Add the ball of ice cream to the glass, letting it roll down the side of the glass. Repeat to add a second scoop.

3 pour in the soda

✳ Pour the seltzer water over the ice cream. It will foam up, so pour slowly.

4 decorate & serve

✳ If you like, top the ice cream soda with a dollop of whipped cream and a cherry.

✳ Serve right away with a straw or long spoon.

more ideas!

root beer float

Add 2 scoops of vanilla ice cream to a large glass or mug. Open one 12-ounce can of cold root beer and slowly pour it over the ice cream. Stop pouring when the foam is just about to flow over the edge of the glass. Serve right away.

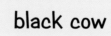

black cow

Drizzle 2 tablespoons chocolate syrup into a tall glass. Add 2 scoops vanilla ice cream. Next, open one 12-ounce can of cold root beer and slowly pour it over the ice cream. Stop pouring when the foam is just about to flow over the edge of the glass. Serve right away.

sherbet float

Add 2 scoops orange, berry, or pineapple sherbet to a tall glass. Slowly pour about ¾ cup cold lemon-lime soda or ginger ale over the sherbet. Serve right away.

use your favorite fruit sherbet for a refreshing treat!

old-fashioned hot cocoa

ingredients

whole milk 1⅓ cups

unsweetened cocoa powder
1 tablespoon

sugar 1 tablespoon

vanilla extract ⅛ teaspoon

mini marshmallows or whipped cream (page 25) for serving

tools

measuring cups & spoons

small saucepan

mug

spoon

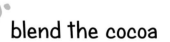

1 warm the milk

✴ Before you start, be sure an adult is nearby to help.

✴ Warm the milk in the saucepan over low heat until tiny bubbles appear around the edges of the pan. Remove from the heat.

2 blend the cocoa

✴ Put the cocoa, sugar, and vanilla in the mug. Stir with the spoon to combine.

✴ Add 1 tablespoon hot milk to the cocoa mixture and stir until it is smooth with no visible lumps.

✴ Ask an adult to help you pour the remaining hot milk into the mug. Stir well, top with the marshmallows or whipped cream, and serve right away.

glossary

This alphabetical list explains many of the words, tools, and ingredients you'll find in this cookbook.

b

bake
To cook foods with hot, dry air in an oven.

baking dish
A deep glass or ceramic dish used for baking or roasting.

baking powder
A white chemical product made by combining baking soda, an acid such as cream of tartar, and cornstarch. Makes doughs and batters rise during baking.

baking sheet
Thin, rectangular metal pan used for baking.

baking soda
A white chemical powder that, when combined with an acidic ingredient such as sour cream or buttermilk, releases carbon dioxide gas, thus causing a batter to rise in the oven.

beat
To mix ingredients vigorously, stirring with a spoon, fork, or beaters in a circular motion.

biscuit cutter
Round metal cutter with a handle attached used to create biscuits or shortcakes.

blend
To combine two or more ingredients thoroughly. Also, to mix ingredients briskly in an electric blender.

blender
Electric appliance used for blending different types of foods, such as milk shakes, frappés, and smoothies.

boil
To heat a liquid until bubbles constantly rise to its surface and break. A gentle boil is when small bubbles rise and break slowly. A rolling boil is when large bubbles rise and break quickly.

box grater-shredder
A tall, 4-sided metal tool covered with different-sized holes and used for grating citrus zest and for shredding cheese.

buckle
A simple layer cake made with fresh fruit.

butter
Butter comes in two forms, salted and unsalted. Many baking recipes call for unsalted butter so that the amount of salt in the recipe can be better controlled.

buttermilk
Type of milk that has "cultures" added to it and is similar to yogurt. It is often used in desserts and baked goods and has a tangy flavor and thick texture.

c

cake stand
Raised stand on which cakes can be easily frosted and then served.

chocolate
Chocolate is available in many forms, including semisweet chocolate, a dark, sweet chocolate sold in blocks, in bars, and as chips; and unsweetened chocolate, a bitter product with a strong chocolate flavor sold in small squares or blocks. Unsweetened cocoa powder is a fine, bitter powder with a strong chocolate flavor.

chop
To cut food into pieces using a sharp knife. Finely chopped pieces are small; coarsely chopped pieces are large.

cinnamon
The bark of a tropical evergreen tree, cinnamon has a mildly sweet flavor. It is available ground or in sticks. Both are sold in jars.

citrus juicer
A shallow bowl with a deeply fluted, inverted cone that fits into a citrus half to easily extract the fruit's juice.

clove
Small spice shaped like a tiny nail with a round head. Its flavor is strong, sweet, and peppery.

cocoa powder
See "chocolate."

coffee powder
Instant coffee sold in jars. It can be dissolved in water and used as a flavoring.

colander
A metal or plastic bowl that is perforated with many small holes and has two handles. A colander is used to rinse fruits before using.

cookie sheet
A flat metal baking pan, usually with a low rim on one or two ends to allow for easily sliding cookies onto a cooling rack.

cooling rack
Made of heavy-duty wire, these square, rectangular, or round racks have small feet that raise them above the countertop. Hot items are placed on top, so that the air circulates on all sides to help the items cool quickly.

cornstarch

A very fine powder made by grinding the center of corn kernels. Used as a thickener.

corn syrup

A thick, sweet syrup made from corn; available in two types, light and dark.

cream cheese

A soft, spreadable cows milk cheese with a mildly tangy flavor. It can be found in a block, or whipped and sold in a tub.

crosswise

In the opposite direction, or perpendicular to, the longest side of a piece of food or a pan.

cupcake liners

Paper liners that fit into the cups of muffin pans to prevent sticking and give the baked goods a pretty look.

d

divide

To split a batch of dough, batter, or ingredients into smaller, equal batches.

dollop

A generous spoonful of a smooth, soft substance such as whipped cream.

drizzle

To pour a liquid back and forth lightly over food in a thin stream.

dry ingredients

The ingredients in a batter or dough that are not liquid. Examples are flour, sugar, salt, baking powder, baking soda, and cocoa powder.

dust

To cover a food, your hands, or a work surface lightly with flour or sugar.

e

electric mixer

A handheld or stand mixer with different speeds that quickly mixes batters and doughs.

extract

Concentrated flavoring made from plants or nuts. Popular extracts for desserts include almond, mint, and vanilla.

f

fine-mesh sieve

A tool used to separate lumps or larger particles of food from smaller ones. It consists of a fine, wire-mesh "bowl" attached to a long handle.

flour, all-purpose

The most common type of flour available, all-purpose flour is composed of a blend of wheats so that it works equally well for cakes, cookies, and other baked goods.

fondue fork

Pronged metal skewer used for dipping small morsels of food into fondue.

fondue pot

A pot used to hold fondue, a dish of melted chocolate or other food presented in a central pot at the table. Eaters use fondue forks to hold small morsels of food, which are dipped into the melted substance and then eaten.

frappé

A creamy, blended drink made from fruit juice and ice cream.

freezerproof

Dishes that can withstand the intense cold of the freezer without damaging them.

frying pan

A shallow pan with sloping sides that is used for sautéing or frying food on the stove top.

g

ginger

Fresh ginger looks like a brown, gnarly root and has a refreshing, sweet flavor. Ground, dried ginger has a peppery flavor.

graham cracker

A whole-wheat, honey-sweetened rectangular cookie often used as crumbs for pie crusts.

grate

To slide an ingredient, such as citrus zest, across a surface of small, sharp-edged holes on a box grater-shredder to create tiny pieces.

grease

To rub a baking pan or baking dish evenly with butter or oil to prevent sticking.

h

heatproof

Dishes, utensils, or surfaces that can come in contact with high heat without damaging them.

heavy cream

Also called heavy whipping cream, heavy cream has a thick, rich consistency because it contains a high percentage of milk fat.

hull

The tough, white center of a strawberry. Also refers to the process of removing the hull by pulling or cutting it out.

i

ice cream paddle

A flat, shovel-shaped metal tool used to remove ice cream from its container or pack it into a new one.

ice cream scoop

A tool used to scoop ice cream into a ball-shaped portion.

invert

To turn a piece of bakeware, usually a pan containing a cake, upside down so that the food falls gently onto a cooling rack or a plate.

k

knife, paring

A small sharp knife for a variety of different uses, including peeling and coring.

knife, serrated

Also called a bread knife, this has a serrated edge that works like a saw to easily cut through hard blocks of chocolate and firm crusts of cake or bread.

knife, sharp

Tool used for slicing, dicing, and chopping all sorts of ingredients. Handle with care!

l

lengthwise

In the same direction as, or parallel to, the longest side of a piece of food or a pan.

line

To cover the bottom of a cake pan, baking sheet, or other pan with parchment paper or aluminum foil to prevent sticking.

loaf dish

A glass dish shaped like a loaf of bread.

m

malted milk powder

A mixture of malt sugar and milk powder used to flavor cold drinks.

melon baller

A small tool with a round metal bowl attached to a handle designed to create melon balls; also useful for scooping chocolate mixtures.

mint

A refreshing herb, popular for many types of desserts and drinks.

muffin pan

Metal baking pan with small indented cups for baking muffins and cupcakes.

mulled

A mulled drink is sweetened and infused with spices and fruit.

n

nutmeg

A fragrant spice ground from the seed of a tropical tree.

o

offset icing spatula

A long utensil consisting of a narrow metal blade that angles off the handle. It is especially helpful when frosting or icing baked goods.

orange oil

Intensely flavored oil made from the zest of oranges.

oven mitts

Thick, heavy-duty cotton gloves that protect hands when handling hot pots or pans.

p

parchment paper

A nonstick, burn-resistant paper used for baking.

pastry bag

A cone-shaped plastic or canvas bag used for applying fillings and frostings. Different decorating tips, such as a plain round tip or a star tip, can be inserted into the bag's hole to create different shapes.

pastry blender

A tool consisting of a row of steel wires attached to a handle to help easily blend butter and flour to make pastry dough.

peel

To strip or cut away the skin or rind from fruits and vegetables.

pie dish

A shallow round glass or ceramic baking dish.

pinch

The amount of a dry ingredient that you can pick up, or "pinch," between your thumb and forefinger; less than $1/8$ teaspoon.

pith

The bitter white part of citrus peel.

poppy seeds

Black, tiny, round seeds used as a topping or filling in desserts and other baked goods.

preheat

To heat an oven to a specific temperature before use.

r

refrigerate

To place food in the refrigerator to chill or to become firm.

rolled oats

Whole oat grains that have been flattened and steamed. Used to make oatmeal and desserts.

rolling pin

A long wooden tool used for rolling out dough.

roll out

To flatten dough with a rolling pin until smooth, even, and usually thin.

room temperature

The temperature of a comfortable room. Baking ingredients are often brought to room temperature so they will soften and blend easily.

s

salt

Salt brings out the flavors of food, even sweet ones! It can be fine grained, like regular salt, or coarse. Rock salt is used for some ice cream makers to keep things extra cold.

saucepan

A pan with tall sides used for stove-top cooking, such as melting chocolate and warming milk.

sauté pan

A shallow pan with straight sides used for cooking food on the stove top.

set

When a filling or a liquid becomes more solid, such as when lemon bars finish baking the filling is "set."

set aside

To put ingredients to one side while you do something else.

sherbet

A frozen dessert made from fruit and a small amount of milk.

simmer

To heat a liquid to just below boiling. The surface of the liquid should be steaming and a few tiny bubbles may form.

skewer

A thin bamboo skewer is used to test cakes and muffins as they are baking.

slice

To cut food lengthwise or crosswise with a knife, forming thick or thin pieces.

slotted spoon

A spoon with holes in it used to remove solid foods from liquid.

soft peak

Whipped cream that forms a peak that gently falls to the side when the whisk or beaters are lifted.

sour cream

A tangy, smooth cream made by making fresh cream sour.

spatula, rubber

A flexible rubber tool attached to a wooden handle for scraping the sides of bowls. Also available are heatproof spatulas made from silicone for scraping hot foods.

spread

To apply a soft item, such as butter or frosting, over another food in an even layer.

stir

To move a spoon, fork, whisk, or other utensil continuously through dry or wet ingredients, usually in a circular pattern.

sugar, brown

A moist blend of granulated sugar and molasses. Brown sugar is sold in two basic types: light (also known as golden) and dark.

sugar, granulated

Small, white granules that pour easily. When a recipe calls for just "sugar," always use granulated sugar.

sugar, powdered

Also called confectioners' sugar, this is granulated sugar finely ground and mixed with a small amount of cornstarch.

sweetened condensed milk

Milk that has most of the water removed from it and is mixed with sugar. It is thick, creamy, and very sweet, and you buy it in a can. This is not the same as evaporated milk.

t

thicken

When a food changes from a loose, liquid consistency to a thick, firmer one.

tongs

Scissor-like tools with blunt ends for grasping food.

trim

To cut food so that it is uniform in size and shape. Also, to cut away any unneeded or inedible part.

truffle

Rich chocolate candy that looks like a fungi with the same name that's found in Europe.

v

vanilla extract

A liquid flavoring made from vanilla beans, the dried pods of a type of orchid.

vanilla syrup

A sweet, thick, vanilla-flavored liquid used to flavor milk shakes, ice cream sodas, and coffee drinks.

vegetable oil

Bland-tasting cooking oil made by blending vegetable-based oils.

vegetable peeler

A small tool used for stripping peels off fruits and vegetables.

w

wet ingredients

The liquid ingredients used in a baking recipe, including water, milk, cream, eggs, and extracts.

whip

To beat a food such as heavy cream using a whisk or electric mixer to increase its volume by beating air into it.

whisk

A whisk is made of loops of sturdy wire that are attached to a handle. To whisk something means to stir a liquid, such as cream, vigorously with a whisk, adding air and thereby increasing its volume.

work surface

A flat space, such as a kitchen counter or a kitchen work table, used for cutting, mixing, or preparing foods.

y

yogurt

A custardlike dairy food with a tart flavor, prepared from milk. Plain yogurt, often used in baking, is unsweetened and unflavored.

z

zest

The thin, brightly colored outer layer or peel of a citrus fruit.

index

ƒP

FREE PRESS

A Division of Simon & Schuster, Inc.
1230 Avenue of the Americas
New York, NY 10020

WILLIAMS-SONOMA

Founder & Vice-Chairman Chuck Williams

WELDON OWEN INC.

Chief Executive Officer John Owen
President and Chief Operating Officer Terry Newell
Chief Financial Officer Christine E. Munson
Vice President International Sales Stuart Laurence
Vice President and Creative Director Gaye Allen
Vice President and Publisher Hannah Rahill
Associate Publisher Sarah Putman Clegg
Senior Editor Jennifer Newens
Art Director and Designer Marisa Kwek
Production Director Chris Hemesath
Color Manager Teri Bell
Production and Reprint Coordinator Todd Rechner

WILLIAMS-SONOMA KIDS IN THE KITCHEN SERIES

Conceived and produced by Weldon Owen Inc.
814 Montgomery Street, San Francisco, CA 94133
Telephone: 415 291 0100   Fax: 415 291 8841

In collaboration with Williams-Sonoma, Inc.
3250 Van Ness Avenue, San Francisco, CA 94109

A WELDON OWEN PRODUCTION

For information regarding special discounts for bulk purchases,
please contact Simon & Schuster Special Sales at 800 456 6798 or
business@simonandschuster.com

Set in AG Schoolbook, Arial, Candy Square, Gill Sans, and Joppa

Color separations by Bright Arts Hong Kong.
Printed and bound in China by SNP Leefung Printers Limited.

First printed in 2006.

10 9 8 7 6 5 4 3 2

Library of Congress Cataloging-in-Publication data is available.

ISBN-13: 978-0-7432-7857-7
ISBN-10: 0-7432-7857-7

Author

CAROLYN BETH WEIL is an accomplished baker with more than
two decades of experience. She was the first pastry chef for
Jeremiah Tower's famed San Francisco restaurant, Stars. Ms. Weil
contributed to *The Baker's Dozen Cookbook,* and is the author of
Pie & Tart and *Fruit Desserts* in the Williams-Sonoma Collection series.
Her articles have appeared in such publications as *The Washington
Post* and *Fine Cooking.* She lives in Berkeley, California, where she
owned a bakery for ten years.

General Editor

CHUCK WILLIAMS, general editor, has helped to revolutionize
cooking in America. He opened his first Williams-Sonoma store in
the California wine country town of Sonoma in 1956, later moving
it to San Francisco. More than 235 stores are now open in the
United States, and the company's catalog boasts an annual
circulation of more than 40 million.

Photographer

JASON LOWE is an award-winning food and travel photographer.
His work has appeared in numerous magazines and cookbooks,
including *Savoring Tuscany; Savoring Provence; Essentials of Grilling;
Kids Baking;* and Foods of the World *Barcelona* and *Florence;* all are
volumes in Williams-Sonoma cookbook series.

ACKNOWLEDGMENTS

Weldon Owen wishes to thank the following people for their generous
support in producing this book: Heather Belt; Geoff, Tara, and Ella Brogan;
Cate Conniff; Ken DellaPenta; Leslie Evans; Sharon Silva; and Sharron
Wood. We would also like to thank our wonderful kid models: Eliza and
Guy Beca; Thomas Bedford; Holly and Maddison Brogan; Jammel Liuaga;
Sasha McEwen; Freddy Riddiford; and Zildjian Talaepa.

recipe list